Raindrops
Fall All Around

by
Charles Ghigna

illustrated by
Laura Watson

raintree
a Capstone company — publishers for children

In the country, in the town ...

rain is falling all around.

Raindrops drip on leaves and flowers.

Cars splash through the April showers.

Raindrops keep a steady beat.

Rain forms puddles in the street.

Rain turns hillsides fresh and green.

Raindrops wash the pavements clean.

A flowing stream fills up with rain.

Rain seeps down into the drain.

Rushing water makes a path.

Bluebirds take a little bath.

Ducklings swim around the lake.

14

Raindrops make the puppies shake.

Lightning flashes in the sky.

Thunder rumbles way up high.

Time to say goodnight to rain.

Raindrops tap-dance on the pane.

Rain clouds slowly pass on by.

A rainbow spreads across the sky.

All about rain

- Rain is a type of precipitation. Precipitation is rain, snow, sleet or hail that falls from clouds to the ground.
- Did you know that the water in a puddle may once have been water in your drinking glass? The water cycle makes this possible. Rain falls from clouds to the ground as part of the water cycle. Have a look at this diagram of a water cycle:

condensation – vapour turns into water

evaporation – water turns into vapour

precipitation – water, snow or ice falls

water collects on the ground

- Tiny raindrops are called drizzle.
- People can measure rainfall with a tool called a rain gauge.
- When a lot of rain falls all at once, flooding can take place. Flooding occurs when water covers what is normally dry land.
- Scientists use tools to help predict weather. To predict means to tell what something may be like in the future.

weather radar station – uses radar to predict weather

anemometer – measures wind speed and wind direction

Titles in this series:

Hail to Spring!

Raindrops Fall All Around

Sunshine Brightens Springtime

A Windy Day in Spring

Websites

www.metoffice.gov.uk/education/kids

Explore the fascinating world of weather through games, experiments, facts and photographs on the Met Office's "For Kids" section of this interactive website.

For Charlotte and Christopher.

Thanks to our adviser for his expertise, research and advice:
Terry Flaherty, PhD, Professor of English

Raintree is an imprint of Capstone Global Library Limited, a company incorporated in England and Wales having its registered office at 7 Pilgrim Street, London, EC4V 6LB – Registered company number: 6695582

www.raintree.co.uk
myorders@raintree.co.uk

Text © Capstone Global Library Limited 2015
The moral rights of the proprietor have been asserted.

Editorial Credits
Shelly Lyons and Elizabeth R. Johnson, editors; Lori Bye, designer; Nathan Gassman, art director; Tori Abraham, production specialist

ISBN 978 1 4062 8865 0
18 17 16 15 14
10 9 8 7 6 5 4 3 2 1

British Library Cataloguing in Publication Data
A full catalogue record for this book is available from the British Library.

Design Elements
The illustrations in this book were created with acrylics and digital collage; Shutterstock: R2D2

Every effort has been made to contact copyright holders of material reproduced in this book. Any omissions will be rectified in subsequent printings if notice is given to the publisher.

All the Internet addresses (URLs) given in this book were valid at the time of going to press. However, due to the dynamic nature of the Internet, some addresses may have changed, or sites may have changed or ceased to exist since publication. While the author and publisher regret any inconvenience this may cause readers, no responsibility for any such changes can be accepted by either the author or the publisher.

Printed and bound in China.